Animales del zoológico / Zoo Animals

ELEFANTES / ELEPHANTS AT THE ZOO

By Finn Ward

Traducido por Ana María García

Gareth Stevens PUBLISHING

Please visit our website, www.garethstevens.com. For a free color catalog of all our high-quality books, call toll free 1-800-542-2595 or fax 1-877-542-2596.

Library of Congress Cataloging-in-Publication Data

Ward, Finn.
Elephants at the zoo = Elefantes / Finn Ward.
pages cm. — (Zoo animals = Animales del zoológico)
Parallel title: Animales del zoológico
In English and Spanish.
Includes index.
ISBN 978-1-4824-3227-5 (library binding)
1. Elephants—Juvenile literature. 2. Zoo animals—Juvenile literature. I. Title.
QL737.P98W367 2016
599.67—dc23

First Edition

Published in 2016 by
Gareth Stevens Publishing
111 East 14th Street, Suite 349
New York, NY 10003

Editor: Ryan Nagelhout
Designer: Katelyn E. Reynolds

Photo credits: Cover, p. 1 Erika Kusuma Wardani/Shutterstock.com; p. 5 My Life Graphic/Shutterstock.com; p. 7 Pecold/Shutterstock.com; p. 9 Mavadee/Shutterstock.com; pp. 11, 24 (ears) canoniroff/Shutterstock.com; p. 13 TJUKTJUK/Shutterstock.com; p. 15 Aleksandra Duda/Shutterstock.com; pp. 17, 24 (zookeeper) ANGELIKA WARMUTH/AFP/Getty Images; p. 19 Blanscape/Shutterstock.com; p. 21 Andrea Izzotti/Shutterstock.com; p. 23 anyaivanova/Shutterstock.com.

Printed in the United States of America

CPSIA compliance information: Batch #CS15GS: For further information contact Gareth Stevens, New York, New York at 1-800-542-2595.

Contenido

Contents

En el zoológico viven
muchos animales.

Many animals live
at the zoo.

¡En algunos zoológicos hay elefantes!

Some zoos have elephants!

¡Los elefantes son enormes!

Elephants are huge!

Sus orejas son muy grandes.

They have very big ears.

Viven en grupos.
Se llaman manadas.

They live in groups.
These are called herds.

Necesitan mucho espacio donde caminar.

They need lots of room to walk.

Hay personas que
cuidan a los elefantes.
Son los guardas
del zoológico.

People care for
zoo elephants.
These are called
zookeepers.

¡A los elefantes les encanta comer!

Elephants love to eat!

Les gusta comer
hierba y fruta.

They like to eat
grass and fruit.

¡A los bebés elefante les encanta jugar!

Baby elephants love to play!

Palabras que debes aprender/ Words to Know

(las) orejas/
ears

(el) guarda del zoológico/
zookeeper

Índice/Index